©2015 Lisa Puerto
All rights reserved
Printed in the United States of America

Living Purple Publishing
8469 S. Van Ness Avenue, #7
Inglewood, CA 90305

ISBN: 978-0-692-38369-8   (Paperback)

Cover Design by Elijah Richard
Co-editor Leah Williams

Published by Living Purple Publishing
No part of this publication may be reproduced, stored in a retrieval system, or transmitted in any form by any means, electronic, mechanical, photocopy, recording, or otherwise without prior written permission of Lisa Puerto, except for brief quotation in publications.

REAL ESTATE 100
The Teen Home Buying Experience

LISA PUERTO

©2015 Lisa Puerto

To all pre-teens and teens who dare to show the world real estate is not just for adults—your home buying experience matters too!

CONTENTS

The Big Deal About This Book 9

Chapter 1:
WHO'S GOT YOUR BACK
Agency Relationships 21

Chapter 2:
GETTIN' YOUR BUCK$ IN ORDER
Financing 37

Chapter 3:
LET THE BUYING & SELLING BEGIN
Escrow 55

Acknowledgments 69
About the Author 75
Tag & Follow   76

THE BIG DEAL ABOUT THIS BOOK

Hey *You*,

You might be wondering why this book even exists and is aimed at young folks like you...*I'll try not to bore you, promise.* As you read through these pages you will see that the subject of home ownership will soon become a dream of yours if not already! I hope to take you from dreaming to what your home would look like to how you will buy that home. I realize those thoughts are two different processes for you right now. The point of all this is to bring to real life the things you will need to know about home buying and real estate. As a matter of fact, because you're reading this book your light-years ahead of your older peers.

When I was in middle school and high school I was not concerned with the financial world around me or adult-like responsibilities, like paying bills, buying a car, working, and even dreaming of becoming a home owner one day. I was too busy with my day-to-day activities like school work, home chores, and hangin' with friends. As you get older, these activities are replaced with studying for a college exam or working *(still school <u>and</u> work);* cooking, cleaning your home *(still home chores);* and updating social networking sites *(and still hangin' with friends).* See the only difference is you're older.

So, I feel it's only fair that you understand some basics about buying a home because you will eventually become old enough to earn a living, build a career, create a family, and want to lay roots in the town in which you live…all the adult stuff soon to come—oh joy!

The key thing to understand is when it's your turn to purchase real estate, know that you don't have to do it the way your parents did. I hope to help you understand important points about buying that so many of your family and friends did not know when they decided to make home ownership a reality. I will refer to *brain implants* as the ideas you already have about home buying from what you may have heard, seen, or read. To be quite honest, in the past few years, the news about real estate has not been all positive. You probably heard the cool stories about people with sudden cash flow and buying all kinds of neat stuff, from cars, boats, housing renovations, other real estate, and the list goes on. This is known as real estate *boom* because the value of real estate goes up. Then you heard the sad stories about people suddenly losing their homes, homes "catching" fire, housing scams, banks closing and that list goes on. This is known as real estate *bust* because the value of real estate goes down. These are basic economics – the economy goes through cycles of boom and bust.

In this book I will label these misconceptions as **"brain implants"** so they're easier to identify when you see them, or you can refer back to this book as a guide when you cross the home buying bridge. At the end of your reading, you should be equipped with the basic understanding of knowing what rights you have as a real estate consumer and be confident when you begin your home buying journey. However, I want this to be your first home buying experience.

You learn how to be consumers by modeling what you see, and so far, your parents/grandparents/uncles/cousins were once children (including myself) that were learning from what their family/friends did or did not do when it involved real estate decisions. The habits we learn continue from generation to generation. Then I realized maybe real estate should be introduced on a personal level, earlier on rather than later in life when all the *brain implanting* has already occurred. See school teaches the basics of reading, math, history, and science. Why? Maybe because you will eventually use them in your daily lives to function as a citizen of this country, or because they're survival tools, right? Same goes for the lessons we learn about real estate. Much of what we see today has tons of real estate history that we overlook. I don't want you to ignore them anymore because when you're an adult you will have to make decisions about them too!

In order to understand the home buying experience as a "First-Time Home Buyer" it's best to start one step before that. Currently, any new home buyer that enters the market would get a crash course in real estate (real estate 101 for Agents) and it can become overwhelming because it's new. I'm suggesting that there be a pre-requisite or a beginner's course to this crash course that starts before you graduate high school, call it "Real Estate

100." Waiting until years later to learn the basics of financial decision making, responsible spending, and conducting business with integrity has got us into micro and macro economic trouble over the years. Therefore, let me be the first to keep it *Real Estate 100*...

Chapter 1
WHO'S GOT YOUR BACK
Agency Relationships

CHAPTER 1
WHO'S GOT YOUR BACK

Agency Relationships

"Everybody Works for Somebody"

Think of this section as getting to know the key players of the real estate game. I won't overkill the part about needing to save to buy a home, because I trust that you already know how to do this. You're strategic in saving for the latest shoes, clothes, and video games. Saving for a major purchase like a home works in the same way. It requires focus and responsible saving and spending, and lots of patience. Look, unless you receive a large monetary inheritance (*a real come-up*), you will need help to purchase a large investment like a home, and often times you will borrow money, or <u>finance</u>, from a bank, credit union, or private creditor, known as <u>lenders</u>. The amount you borrow and pay back to the lender in smaller payments over a set amount of time is called a <u>mortgage</u>. Also, make note that borrowing money is not free—lenders will charge you a <u>fee</u>, or a cost to borrow their money, this is known as <u>interest</u>. The money you save, known as your <u>down payment</u>, plus the amount you borrow will add up to the total amount you can use to purchase a home, called <u>purchasing power</u>.

    Don't worry about the amount needed to save, there are many programs that can help you purchase, but having a good amount (3%-5%) of money set aside really gives you the upper hand when it comes to buying what you desire in size and style of your home. Remember when you priced the newest video game console or shoes; you knew exactly how much to save in order to buy it. Well buying a home works the same way. When you start your search, most likely an internet search, you will have an idea of how much money you need to buy a home.

There are great advantages to understanding this section when you start your home buying experience, mainly because you get to choose who is on your side!

Believe it or not, most adults don't realize they can choose who works for them. Whether they are selling a home or buying one. So here are the players: Buyer, Seller, and Real Estate Agent(s), and yes there can be more than one agent during a home buying transaction or sale. Your real estate agent acts as your personal coach making the calls but **not** without your input first!

> Tip: Do a little detective work on your agent. Look up the name or license # of any agent to see if they have any violations, check license status, etc. Visit the Department of Real Estate website for your state. For example, California residents can visit www.bre.ca.gov to learn more.

Which leads me to **Brain implant #1**: "Buyers have to pay for Agent Representation." Nope. Not true. This is referred to as Buyer Representation, and this is not <u>always</u> true. The Buyer's Agent is paid through a shared commission (payment) already set by the Seller's Agent. For example, *You* hire a real estate agent to be on your side to help you search and find a home; prepare a contract the way you want to buy a home and for how much, known as a <u>Purchase Contract Offer</u>.

If the Seller accepts your Offer, then the Seller's real estate agent will pay your agent for your accepted offer. Payment occurs once all the terms or set agreements in the contract have been completed; this process is called <u>close of escrow</u>.

In real estate, you as a buyer or seller are required to understand who works for whom in a real estate transaction. The reason is because the agent owes you a higher sense of responsibility in trust and loyalty as your agent. Meaning, they are expected to have your best interest first above all else <u>and</u> everyone else. *So be sure to know who's got your back.*

Have you ever paid attention to those open house signs in your neighborhood? Maybe knocked over a few on your way to school or store just to be funny, or turned the sign in the opposite direction to mislead folks from finding the house…seriously avoid the temptation. (Although, it's funny when you think about it ☺) Jokes aside, there is another popular brain implant about open house—**Brain implant #2**: "Open House Agent is also the Seller's Agent." False! The reason this is inaccurate and important to know is because the agent that holds the home open for a courtesy showing to the public, often times is someone like me. Someone who loves to engage buyers about what they should know about the home buying experience. Often times, I'm not working for the seller when I do this. This is a fun time for me because I get to meet and greet folks like yourselves that come in with your family or friends, and you're just as curious as they are about what's inside the home. Someone like me greets you with a warm and inviting smile, and is ready to answer any questions you might have. The cool thing is that you are not shy to ask me questions, and you indeed ask great questions that sometimes your older folks will not or would not ask me. For this reason I am confident in you and **You are ready** to know this subject.

    What's interesting and sad about the next misconception is that so many people

believe it—**Brain implant #3**: "The Seller's Agent won't work with my Agent." Yikes! Say's who? No way, not true! Can you tell this one makes me cringe, ugh. It's like buying a two-player video game, and then telling the second player that you have to use one controller to play, huh? Can you see how that would be problematic, almost unfair, right?

I agree. That's why you should know that the Seller can choose whomever they would like to represent them, and you have those same rights as a buyer. Don't feel intimated that the other side won't want to play (or sell) because you brought your own coach to the game. It actually creates a level and fair playing field. Game on!

Chapter 2
GETTIN' YOUR BUCK$ IN ORDER
Financing

Chapter 2
GETTIN' YOUR BUCK$ IN ORDER

Financing

"Where to get it and why is it important"

Have you ever walked into a store and started dropping all kinds of stuff into your cart that you knew you just had to have; and then when you got to the cash register you realized you didn't have enough to pay for everything in your cart? Not a good feeling right? You either had to put some items back, or just canceled your order altogether. (I've been there, totally un-cool when there's a long check-out line). It baffles me that some adults shop first before they know for sure what they can afford. You don't want to do this when you start the process of buying your home. Preparing to buy your home should be handled with attention and precise details to the money aspects of purchasing.

By the time you are ready to work out the money matters, you would have saved for a down payment and are ready to seek additional funding from a lender. It's best to know your shopping limits before you start shopping. There's a very simple way to taking out the guess work of how much you should be spending on your home. Remember, earlier in the intro' I mentioned about paying bills? Well your home mortgage will be one of those regular bills, and there's a very simple formula to follow (don't worry I'm not going to make you learn some complicated real estate formula, promise). The monthly payments of your home should not be more than one-third (1/3) of your monthly income (money earned). For example, you earn $4,500 each month. You take $4,500 and multiply it by 1/3, which equals $1,500, see <u>Ex 1</u>. This means $1,500 is the amount your monthly home payments <u>should not exceed</u>. Easy, right? Don't worry about the calculations and other factors involved in financing[1], there's actually a professional you can hire to help you with this.

> <u>Ex. 1</u>: $4,500 (income) × 1/3 (limit)
> = $1,500, monthly home payment

---

[1] *There are a lot more technical terms to learn like points, origination fees, APR, etc, you can email me at info@realestate100.net to learn more*

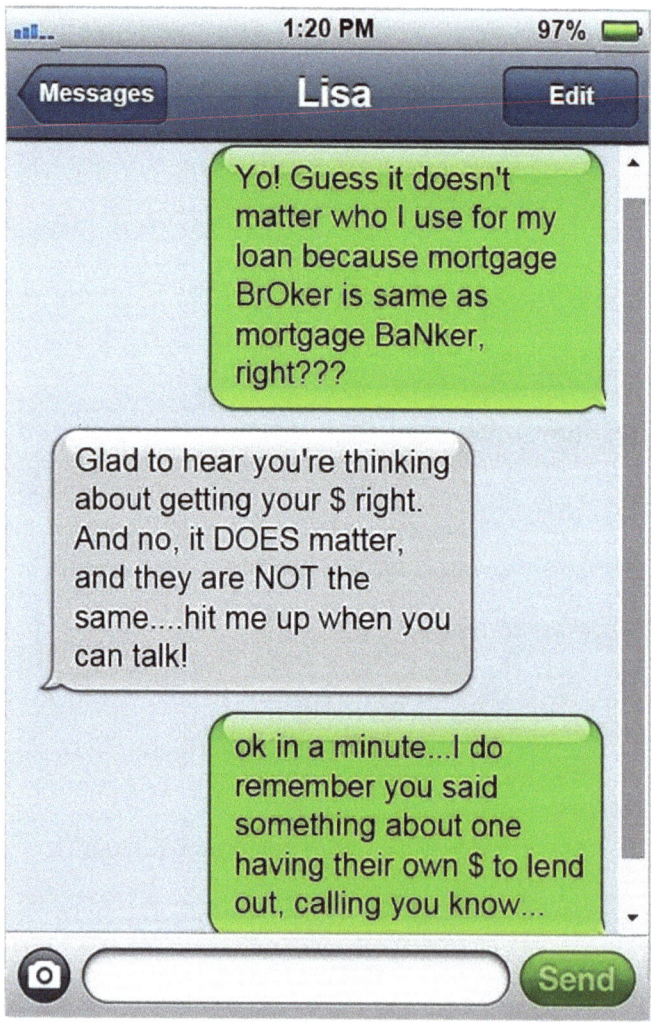

Brain implant #4: "Mortgage Broker is the same as a Mortgage Banker." Very untrue. There is yet another advantage to this real estate game because you get to choose another team player who will work for you. This is all a part of getting your *bucks in order* (not your ducks ☺), and your choices are either a Mortgage Broker or Mortgage Banker.

It's very important to understand the differences between these additional game players. The mortgage broker is someone that will help "shop" for financing from different lenders or in some cases will lend funds from their own broker-controlled funds and often times sell to larger financial institutions. Mortgage brokers can and do charge you a fee for helping you find a lender who will actually provide the additional money you need to buy your home. Mortgage brokers normally assist buyers that would likely be unable to get a loan from a direct lender because of a problematic credit history. This assistance adds to the overall cost of borrowing money from a direct lender.

Mortgage Bankers work directly for a direct lender that will provide you with funding. A mortgage banker can provide different scenarios to what may be the best type of loan for you. The lender estimates provided to you are based on their specific requirements to qualify for their

> Tip: The amount the lender approves for you to borrow does not mean you have to spend it all. It's just an amount available to you. Remember your shopping cart?

loan programs. Ultimately the decision is yours to make.

I like to remind my clients that life after buying a home should be the same before buying. Meaning, if you borrow the maximum amount the lender approves, then the life you were used to, for example: going to the movies, shopping, eating out, may have to be limited or cut-out altogether. That's no fun and this home buying dream quickly becomes a nightmare! Have you ever heard mom or dad say in frustration *"no we can't go out to eat tonight!"* or *"...I don't have any money for that!"* Sometimes, life can become a bit hectic when you've overextended yourself, and being indebted (owing) to someone will always have that effect on you. Be smart about making financial decisions. You don't have to model the choices you've seen (if negative ones), because after all—these are your choices to make when it's your turn to make them.

Once you've decided who will help with financing (mortgage broker or mortgage banker) you will be asked to provide documentation about how much money you earn, down payment saved, and a copy of your credit report. Credit reports are an important part of financing because it provides a snapshot of how well you have managed your money up until that point. You will hear a lot more about credit scores and credit reports when you're ready to rent an apartment, buy a cell phone, finance a car, etc.

Credit reports are similar to your school progress reports in that they track how you're doing on a specific subject called "money management." If the lender determines you are eligible for a loan, they will provide a conditional pre-approval letter. If you are not approved at this time, the lender will make recommendations to what would improve your loan scenario and eligibility for next time.

A common brain implant among buyers regarding this piece of letter is **Brain implant #5**: "Pre-qualified is the same as Pre-approved." Not knowing that this is a big fat false can cost you big in time and money. A mortgage broker who is not a direct lender, can gather information about your earnings, savings, and credit report and provide a pre-qualification letter. However, this letter does not say that you will actually be provided money to purchase a home. It just means you *might* be eligible for a specified amount. If you were to take this letter and present it with an offer, it's just the same as filling your shopping cart without having any money to pay once you get to the register. *Don't make this mistake.*

Whereas if you complete a loan application, provide all the information I mentioned above to a direct lender, and you're considered as a good candidate for a loan, then the lender can provide a conditional loan pre-approval. This is just as good as having money in the bank when your shopping cart is full and you're ready for check-out. Having this piece of paper will let your real estate agent and the seller of a property know you've got your bucks in order.

Don't be misled into thinking your financing is guaranteed because it's not! The final guarantees come during the escrow process and are finalized when all requirements are met by you and the terms of the accepted Purchase Offer. This is the time you should be paying close attention to any documents you receive from your lender. Also be sure to confirm with your mortgage broker or mortgage banker to show you where in your documents does it state the terms of your loan, interest, and payments, including any mortgage broker or lender fees.

I expect you to use your skills in comparison shopping when you're deciding on the best mortgage for your purchase. This is the part where many folks get confused and easily misled. The lending industry has changed so much over the years and continues to change. It is now much easier to understand the costs between different loan programs offered by competing lenders. (At least, that was the intent.)

> **Tip:** Remember that hiring a Mortgage Broker or Mortgage Banker to help with financing means they work for you and should have your best interest

Let your agent and mortgage broker or mortgage banker explain, or even draw pictures to make this point clear. Otherwise, the rest of the buying experience can become hectic. Remember the team you chose is there to help you.

Chapter 3
LET THE BUYING & SELLING BEGIN
Escrow

Chapter 3

LET THE BUYING & SELLING BEGIN

Escrow

"In the real estate game the best deals benefit all players"

You've got all your team players, your money is in order, and you've found the perfect home. It's time to make an offer to purchase. This will require negotiating the right terms and price to purchase. Your real estate agent helps you with the contract terms, and don't be shy to ask questions when you're not clear about something. For some reason, adults lose this natural-born curiosity that they once had when they were your age. At the time of writing your offer you will write a check for your Good Faith Deposit. It's optional (*unless your are participating in a specific home-buying program*), but having a check for a portion of your down payment shows the Seller that you are serious, and you can back-up what your offer says. You may have heard the saying "Put your money where your mouth is..." (well same idea). Once you have presented an offer to a seller of a property, and your offer is accepted, the tournament games begin.

It depends on the state as to whether an escrow holder or real estate attorney would act as a neutral party to this transaction. Either way, the purpose of escrow is to make sure that all the terms of the contract/offer are carried out by each player. One important part of your contract terms is a saying I've coined called "P-CHI," *pee-chee*. When you were writing your offer with your agent, always make sure to tell them you want to make it "*P-CHI*." This is an acronym for "Purchase Contingent to Home Inspection." By having this important <u>clause</u> (condition) in your offer means you have told the seller that your offer depends on the results and findings of a home inspection paid by you and approved by you.

In other words, you want to know what you're getting before you move forward with a commitment to buy it. Another common misconception about a home inspection is **Brain implant #6**: "Pre-sale home inspections are Optional." From what I've said your guess might be that it *is* optional if you are paying for it, right? Wrong. There are different types of pre-sale home inspections which includes city inspections that must be completed before <u>close of escrow</u>, or the transfer of the property from seller to buyer. Depending on the city where the property is located, there are city laws that require this "buyer-beware" report. For example, this inspection report might uncover illegal additions (like an extra bathroom that was added near the kitchen without permits, missing/faulty smoke detectors, improper installation of windows, and the list goes on with bad repairs/improvements).

The buyer and seller may negotiate who would be responsible for payment of this type of city inspection as well as who would be responsible for fixing the issues uncovered in the inspection report.

> 🎵Tip: You can choose your own Home Inspectors, but <u>NOT</u> your City Inspectors.

If you decide at this point in the game that you do not want to move forward with buying the home because the home inspection reports uncovered more issues than you can financially handle or the seller is not willing to repair, then you can cancel your agreement to purchase. You're within your rights to do so, refer back to P-CHI. Most often buyers aren't sure about this part of canceling a contract and worry about **Brain implant #7**: "The Seller can keep my deposit if I don't buy the home." Whoa! Sooo not true *on* so many levels...

The best part of breaking down the truth about Brain implant #1 is that you learned before you got to this point that a Buyer's Agent is on your team to help you and advise you through this experience. It is your Agent's responsibility and duty to be able to enter you into a purchase contract that you can legally walk away from without losing your good faith deposit, or money.

If you decide to stay in the game, then what happens after inspections and/or repair negotiations goes quickly. Your lender finalizes the terms of the loan for the amount you will borrow to purchase the home, and in real estate we have a very special day that is long awaited called "D-Day" aka "Docs Day." Agents, Title Officers, Escrow Officers, Lenders, Processors, Underwriters (all tournament players) take their places to tie in the exchange between Buyer and Seller. You will be called upon to sign a final packet of documents that includes the transfer title and loan information.

It authorizes the lender to pay for the home on your behalf, transfer title (trust deed) gets recorded with the county recorders' office and you are officially the *Owner*!

> *Tip:* Buyers can choose to legally cancel a contract and keep rights to their deposit. Refer back to your offer and conditions.

Congratulations, you just bought your first home/real estate, and you did it knowing what traps to avoid and mistakes not to make. It will be an emotional purchase, but at least you won't have the added stress of not knowing what to expect. You've covered the very basics in school, like learning to read and solving math problems, now you can add this to your record.

When you're ready to make this dream come true, reflect back to the brain implants and tips in this book to refresh your memory. You will do tons of on-line research, more information overload, and then you will realize it's tough to filter out the accurate information from the false.

> **Tip: Be sure you understand what you're signing.**

Typically house-hunting begins **before** you call an agent, so after much research you will contact an agent that can help you with this initial part of the game. Look for an agent who is transparent. Look for someone who is open to answering questions and sharing information that you did not already know.

Ask questions, be proactive, and be reassured you will find *someone you can trust.* Happy House-Conquering!

Lisa Puerto

Lisa Puerto, Super Agent

ACKNOWLEDGMENTS

I would like to thank Creator GOD for this creative assignment of lending my voice and experience to the youth community. It has been an honor to be used in such a way to reach out to young thinkers, dreamers, and believers.

I would also like to thank my daughter Leah for her inspiration and constant reminders to "break-it-down" to her level. Leah, you have been the very best "open house" buddy. You critiqued me on my presentations, posture, and we made fun of each other while waiting for buyers. You made holding open house fun, thank you! I wish to thank my son Leithen for the joy and happiness he adds to my life, and the reminder of what a bright future we are all responsible for creating in our children. Linden, I would like to thank you for our children and our journey.

I would also like to thank the women in my life who have been *super agents* in their own ways: *Gramma* Sheila Puerto, my mommy Cristina Puerto, Elvinia Williams, and Joshia Puerto. You are not selfish in your being and you do so faithfully from the moment you open your eyes to the very moment you close them. You are caretakers and workers for GOD, reaching those in need. I love you dearly.

I want to give a special thanks to Jorge "G"Horta and Andrew Williams for being men that have supported my career in the ways that you have.

I want to say a word to my brother Javier Beltran and sister Angelique Horta: To be the best that GOD asks you to be, I love you deeply. To Brittney Williams and Andrew Jr "June" Williams: Thank you for your support and continued love of your niece and nephew. I love you all as my siblings.

Also sending love to all my cousins Ronnie, Maya, their mother and my auntie Martha; my cousins William and Alexander and their mother, my auntie Vianney; my nephews Anthony, Ashton, Aidan, Jonathan and their mother Jenny. Manuel Mario my hope is that you see the King within for your legacy which includes Alexis, Autumn, and Emmanuel. And my young Princess Malaya and Prince Jomari I love you! I have written thinking of all of you as the future and know you will take part of something great in your own ways.

A special thanks to my new, current, and future clients who all have a special place in my heart. To Erik & Cindy Nunez, who have paved the way for their own families and have set the home buying experience as a rite of passage. I commend you for your steps and trusting me again and again, oh and did I say *again*, as your *Super Agent*.

To Damien Shampine who showed me your purpose, your greatness, your spirit, thereby allowing me to see mine, *Namaste*, and for that and much more, I am forever grateful and love you from my Soul. To your daughter Jada and son Damien Jr, may you both realize your greatness within and know it to be true. Love you as my own.

And last, but certainly not least, I wish to express great gratitude to all young thinkers for being bold and daring in reading about a subject matter that so many might feel is way above your understanding. But it is meant for you to *overstand.* Continue to think, dream, and believe. Your world is what you envision it to be. You should know that you can make a positive difference in the real estate experience now and in the future. *Keep it Real Estate 100!*

ABOUT THE AUTHOR

Lisa Puerto is a Real Estate Professional, Speaker, and Author. As an advocate of consumer awareness and a proponent of youth empowerment and development, she continues to strive for creative and innovative ways to be a specialized resource for her community and clients.

To learn more about Puerto and request that she speak at a workshop/webinar for your company, group, association, or school please send an email to info@realestate100.net or call (323) 488-3265 for scheduling.
www.realestate100.net
CalBRE # 01736957

**TAG & FOLLOW
@REALESTATE100
#REALESTATE100**

Join the movement by following @realestate100 on Instagram and @TeenRealEstate on Facebook. Show your support and post your real estate goals, questions, and favorite landmarks by tagging @realestate100 and #realestate100.

To learn more about the #REALESTATE100 movement and Lisa Puerto, Super Agent visit the website, www.realestate100.net

ABOUT THIS BOOK

"Real Estate 100" navigates adolescents through the basic steps of home ownership and uncovers the 7 common misconceptions or "brain implants" during the real estate game. New generations of real estate savvy teens become prepared about real estate terms and concepts through true-false questions and funny text message illustrations.

Class is in session!